BEARING WITNESS

GENOCIDE AND ETHNIC CLEANSING IN THE MODERN WORLD™

THE KHMER ROUGE'S GENOCIDAL REIGN IN CAMBODIA

ZOE LOWERY AND SEAN BERGIN

ROSEN
PUBLISHING

NEW YORK

Published in 2017 by The Rosen Publishing Group, Inc.
29 East 21st Street, New York, NY 10010

Library of Congress Cataloging-in-Publication Data

Names: Lowery, Zoe, author. | Bergin, Sean, 1968- author.
Title: The Khmer Rouge's genocidal reign in Cambodia : Zoe Lowery and Sean
  Bergin.
Other titles: Bearing witness (Rosen Publishing Group)
Description: New York : Rosen Publishing, 2017. | 2017 | Series: Bearing
  witness : genocide and ethnic cleansing in the modern world | Includes
  bibliographical references and index.
Identifiers: LCCN 2015050272 | ISBN 9781477785720
Subjects: LCSH: Cambodia—History—20th century. | Genocide—Cambodia. | Pol
  Pot. | Parti communiste du Kampuchea.
Classification: LCC DS554.8 .L69 2016 | DDC 959.604—dc23
LC record available at http://lccn.loc.gov/2015050272

Manufactured in China

CONTENTS

It wasn't until 1944 that the word "genocide" was coined to refer to the intentional killing of a whole group of people. First used by Raphael Lemkin, the term was officially defined in 1948 by the United Nations (UN), after Nazi Germany, during World War II (1939–1945), exterminated six million Jews alone, as well as another six million minorities. The UN was determined to thwart any chances of such horrific, state-sponsored mass murder from ever happening again, so it wrote the Convention on the Prevention and Punishment of the Crime of Genocide. This document defined genocide as "acts committed with intent to destroy, in whole or in part, a national, ethnical, racial, or religious group," whether it is by way of murder, physical or psychological trauma, or preventing reproduction. On December 9, 1948, the UN General Assembly formally approved it, which meant that all member nations were required to comply and punish anyone—leaders or individuals—who disregarded it.

Genocide was hardly a new issue in the twentieth century. All kinds of people all over the globe have been in conflict with one another since the beginning of time. And sometimes this resulted in them massacring innocent civilians. By the time the twentieth century rolled around, developments in technology enabled humans to be annihilated more effectively than ever. Entire towns and cities could be completely destroyed, sometimes in mere hours, thanks to machine guns, automatic weapons, tanks, bombs, chemical and biological weapons, flamethrowers, and other weaponry.

Unfortunately, even after the approval of the UN Convention on Genocide, the horrors of genocide remain quite real.

In some cases the worldwide community has been unwilling or unable to recognize or admit genocide when it occurs. And even after the facts reveal the atrocities to be true, it has failed to bring its criminals to justice. Just look at the horrific Cambodian genocide, which remains scarcely examined, at best, to this day. Yet close to two million Cambodians (around 20 percent of the country's people) died at the hands of the militant dictator Pol Pot and the Khmer Rouge Communist government. Innocent Cambodians were murdered, starved, and tortured.

The Khmers were the prevailing ethnic group in Cambodia, making up 80 percent of the country's people. Pol Pot was a

A memorial to the Cambodian genocide in a former Khmer Rouge prison in Phnom Penh, Cambodia, lists the names of more than twelve thousand victims who died during this horrific time.

Khmer. He went on to completely restructure Cambodia's society with violence and cruelty as well as a goal of cleansing the country of foreign influence and "taints," any blood that was not Khmer. He also put into practice a radical Communist agrarian structure. Pol Pot victimized ethnic Vietnamese, Thai, and Chinese Cambodians. Cities were emptied, and their inhabitants were moved to the country, where they had to perform strenuous agricultural work. He and the Khmer Rouge uplifted the humble Khmer peasant as the country's model, while killing anyone who could not acclimate to the forced labor and eradicating ethnic and religious minorities. Finally, he inexplicably exterminated hundreds of thousands of ethnic Khmers. His horrific actions resulted in the coining of a new term to refer to the mass murder of one's own people: "autogenocide."

Although Pol Pot is now dead, he never stood a real trial or spent a day in prison to make reparation for his ghastly crimes. Most who worked closely with him have also evaded paying for their crimes, although in 2011 several were tried for their part in the genocide. Cambodia is slowly shuffling toward democracy, but poverty makes its achievement slow. The fields once devastated by Pol Pot—known as the Killing Fields—are still littered with the bones of almost two million people. There is one small sliver of hope: in 2013, together with Cambodia's National Assembly, Prime Minister Hun Sen approved a bill that makes it illegal to deny that the genocide, or its atrocities, occurred.

CHAPTER 1

CAMBODIA'S HARD-WON INDEPENDENCE

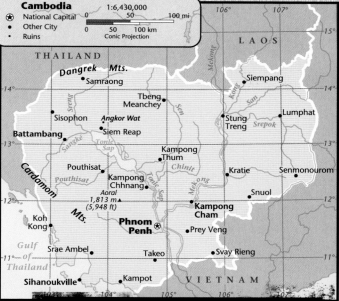

Cambodia
★ National Capital
• Other City
· Ruins
1:6,430,000
0   50   100 mi
0   50   100 km
Conic Projection

THAILAND

LAOS

VIETNAM

Dangrek Mts.
Samraong
Tbeng Meanchey
Sisophon
Angkor Wat
Siem Reap
Battambang
Tonle Sap
Kampong Thum
Pouthisat
Kampong Chhnang
Aoral
1,813 m
(5,948 ft)
Koh Kong
Phnom Penh
Kampong Cham
Prey Veng
Gulf of Thailand
Srae Ambel
Takeo
Svay Rieng
Sihanoukville
Kampot
Siempang
Lumphat
Stung Treng
Srepok
Kratie
Senmonourom
Snuol
Cardamom Mts.

The Angkorean empire was centered over today's northwestern Cambodia and included the present-day countries of Laos, Thailand, and Vietnam.

Between the ninth and fifteenth centuries, in what was known as the Angkorean empire—also known as the Khmer empire or the Kambuja kingdom—Cambodia experienced its golden age. The empire was centered in what is known as northwestern Cambodia today and fanned out to include sections of the modern-day countries of Laos, Thailand, and Vietnam. Its kings lived in the capital, the Angkor area. This area covered more than 100 square miles (259 square kilometers), and several million residents made their home there. It may have been the world's largest preindustrial city.

7

This Angkor temple, a Buddhist monastery and university in the twelfth century, still stands deep in the jungle, centuries after the empire fell to Thai forces.

Yet the Angkorean empire began to fall into decline as Thai forces began to harass the region. By the mid-fifteenth century the Thai kingdom of Ayutthaya had seized the capital region. Within a short period of time, the ever-encroaching jungle reclaimed Angkor, shrouding it in a dense tangle of creeping greenery.

FRENCH PROTECTION

What followed was four hundred years of repeated attacks, invasions, and domination by both Vietnam and Thailand. In 1863, the Cambodian king Norodom, who had been installed by Thai overlords, requested French protection. France had established colonial outposts in neighboring parts of Southeast Asia and promptly accepted Norodom's invitation to administer what it called Cambodge. In English, this was translated as both Kampuchea and Cambodia (all of these names referred to the Kambuja kingdom of Cambodia's golden age).

France was beginning to build a powerful series of colonies throughout Southeast Asia, known collectively as French Indochina. It included Cambodia, Laos, and Vietnam. Cambodia's new "protector" quickly began to seize control of its rice, corn, fish, timber, and rubber plantations, as well as its tobacco, silk, and cotton textile industries. France exported these natural resources and products, taxed both the peasants who harvested them and the merchants who exported them, and collected the profits.

France also took charge of Cambodia's foreign affairs, economy, and defense. The French provided the government, bureaucracy, language, and armed forces. They imported Vietnamese to fill civil-service positions and provide skilled labor. Merchants and shopkeepers were often Chinese. Most Cambodians merely existed, it would seem, to labor in the fields, provide agricultural exports for France, pay taxes to their colonial masters, and suffer from malnutrition and hunger. It was as if they were guest workers in their own country. Even King Norodom was given no real power other than as a symbolic figurehead.

While Cambodian unrest and outright revolts were few and far between during the French colonial period, France's colonies in Vietnam were experiencing similar hardships, and their resentment did begin to boil over into rebellion. This took the form of a series of assassinations of colonial officials and large-scale peasant revolts. Most troubling, from the French perspective, was the formation of the Indochinese Communist Party (ICP), in 1930. Though dominated by Vietnamese leadership, the ICP began to attract growing numbers of Cambodians who were belatedly beginning to feel stirrings of nationalist fervor and anticolonial resentment.

With the outbreak of World War II in 1939, France was overrun by Germany. The French authorities in Cambodia were now too distracted, isolated, and overwhelmed to properly attend to Cambodia's interests. Germany had granted its ally Japan effective control over Indochina. In turn, Japan allowed the French to retain token control over most of Cambodia, but real power and authority had shifted to the Japanese. The French colonial rulers, long accustomed to setting up puppet Cambodian kings, had become puppets themselves.

PATRIOTISM AND LIBERATION INCREASE

In 1941, during World War II, the French chose Prince Norodom Sihanouk to succeed his grandfather, King Monivong.

As the war began to draw to its bloody close, France was liberated from Nazi Germany's occupation by Allied troops, and its colonial officials once again began to exert control over Indochina. The kingdoms had changed in their absence, however. Their brief taste of semi-independence from France during World War II had reignited the nationalist spark for many Cambodians. Pride mingled with shame as Cambodians contemplated how far their culture had fallen and how subservient and dependent they

King Norodom Sihanouk (1922–2012) ruled Cambodia in many capacities: king (twice), prime minister, exiled leader, and president.

had become. They became determined to halt this slide into dependence and victimization and began to greatly mistrust and resent foreign interference in their affairs.

STRANGE AND CHARISMATIC

It was into a chaotic time that Saloth Sar renamed himself Pol Pot and first entered the roiling stream of historic events. In him was crystallized the Cambodians' weight of tragic history and their blossoming hatred—for the French, for all foreign interference, for ineffective and self-serving royalty, for their Vietnamese and Thai neighbors, and for all things non-Khmer and untraditional. Yet concentrated in this one strange and charismatic man, the collective rage of an entire nation would prove impossible to control or contain, and all of Cambodia would become the ultimate victim.

All of these crosscurrents combined to sweep away French colonial rule over Cambodia. Communist guerrillas in northern Vietnam known as the Viet Minh had led the resistance to Japanese forces during the war and stoked nationalist fervor. Following Japan's surrender, they began agitating against renewed French rule, as did some nationalist Khmer forces. By 1953, King Sihanouk had converted to the rapidly growing Cambodian independence movement and began to campaign for the withdrawal of the French. The next year, following a devastating loss at the hands of the Viet Minh in the battle of Dien Bien Phu in Vietnam, France granted Cambodian independence. Norodom Sihanouk was now the undisputed leader of a sovereign nation. His satisfaction at this turn of events would be short-lived, however, as Cambodia was about to be torn apart by a Communist-inspired civil war.

CHAPTER 2

THE PROGRESSION OF POL POT

Saloth Sar (1925–1998) would change his name to Pol Pot and go on to become one of the twentieth century's most terrible tyrants.

Once upon a time there was a little boy who seemed to enjoy a calm, peaceful childhood. But he would grow up to become one of the world's most vicious leaders: Pol Pot. In all likelihood, Saloth Sar, as he was named, was born in March 1925, however some less reliable French colonial records suggest the date to be May 25, 1928. His parents were both ethnic Khmers. Phen Saloth, his father, farmed the land in the village of Prek Sbauv, which is about 90 miles (145 km) north of Phnom Penh, Cambodia's capital. His farming was so successful that he had the largest tile-roofed house in Prek Sbauv.

PRIVILEGED YET ORDINARY

Saloth Sar's family was prosperous, and he was spared working in the fields. He never knew hunger or hard labor, and he received a good education. Through several family members, he even had useful connections to the Royal Palace in Phnom Penh. These royal connections allowed Saloth Sar to leave his humble village behind, travel to Phnom Penh, and attend a Buddhist monastery favored by the royal court. After a year there, he began attending an elite Catholic primary school, the Ecole Miche. Its teachers were French and Vietnamese, and lessons were given in French. This kind of education was usually reserved for French nationals and aristocratic Cambodians. Most ordinary Cambodians received no primary education at all.

By the time Saloth Sar completed his studies at the Ecole Miche (1937–1942) and the equally elite secondary school College Sihanouk (1942–1947), he seemed to have made no impression on his fellow students. He was remembered as a bland, quiet, polite boy who was average in every way and a mediocre, unmotivated student. In 1948, he failed a crucial exam that would have admitted him to the upper classes of the Lycée Sisowath, a select secondary school that would graduate many of Cambodia's future Communist leaders. Rather than continuing his studies with his far more accomplished and ambitious classmates, Saloth Sar enrolled in a technical school just outside Phnom Penh. There, he studied carpentry, widely regarded by faculty and students as the easiest of its subjects.

Though in many respects this turn of events could be considered a humiliation for a former member of the privileged class, Saloth Sar actually began to thrive at the technical school. His new efforts paid off almost immediately. In 1949, he studied for and passed an exam that earned him a scholarship to study radio electronics at an engineering school in France. Quite suddenly, Saloth Sar had reentered the elite, becoming one of only about two hundred Cambodians ever to be sent overseas for education and training.

THE QUIET STUDENT

At College Norodom Sihanouk, the high school Saloth Sar attended in the city of Kompong Cham, the future Pol Pot made little impression on most of his classmates. David P. Chandler, author of *Brother Number One: A Political Biography of Pol Pot*, spoke to several of Saloth Sar's classmates: "'His manner was straightforward, pleasant, and very polite,' one of them said. Another recalled that Sar 'thought a lot, but said very little,' while a third noted that he spent much of his spare time playing basketball and soccer: 'He was a pretty good player, but not outstanding.' Saloth Sar seemed to have no clear ambitions. He was content to drift along, enjoying his companions without making a strong impression on them, secure in the knowledge that he was among friends..."

ENTHRALLED BY COMMUNISM

Saloth Sar arrived in Paris on October 1, 1949. It was a city enthralled by Communism, the strongest French political party of the time. Saloth Sar's political awareness was stimulated and nurtured by his friendship with fellow Cambodian students who had become Communists. In his second year of study in Paris, he began attending political debates and discussions hosted by these friends. Some participants remember Saloth Sar as being an exceptionally articulate and passionate leader of these discussions, while others can barely remember his presence, which they say was sporadic.

Regardless of his true level of involvement in these student gatherings, by 1952, Saloth Sar had become a member of the Communist Party of France. In response to a growing combined Communist and pro-democracy movement in Cambo-

Communist supporters gather in France. While in Paris, Saloth Sar's politics were heavily influenced by the strong Communist Party there, especially that of other Cambodian students.

dia, King Norodom Sihanouk dissolved the National Assembly, arrested members of opposition political parties, and declared martial law. Communists, nationalists, and the Cambodian students in Paris were all outraged and motivated to action. Indeed, even Saloth Sar, ordinarily so passive and reluctant to apply himself or stand out, was inspired to get actively involved in the Communist struggle to "liberate" Cambodia.

Having failed out of school and lost his scholarship, Saloth Sar could not stay in Paris much longer. He returned to Phnom Penh in January 1953, just as King Norodom Sihanouk was trying to stave off nationalist and Communist rebellion by personally urging the French to grant Cambodia its independence.

Once back in Cambodia, Saloth Sar quickly met up with Viet Minh forces of the Indochinese Communist Party (ICP) entrenched near the Vietnamese border. The ICP was aggressively recruiting Cambodians to form all-Khmer guerrilla units and militias. By late 1953, the ICP controlled about one-third of Cambodian territory and as much as one-half of its population. Its sister organization, the Khmer People's Revolutionary Party (KPRP), was also growing rapidly with ICP sponsorship and successfully recruiting Cambodian peasants and former Buddhist monks.

LIBERATION AND CALM

As a member of the French Communist Party, Saloth Sar was accepted into the ICP. The Communist forces escalated their rebellion, and soon France accepted the fact that it could no longer hold onto Indochina without prolonged war, great loss of life, and diminishing economic value. At the Geneva Conference of 1954, France relinquished all claims to Indochina. To quell fighting, it was decided that Vietnam would be divided into two halves—a Communist north and non-Communist south—until national elections could be held. Viet Minh forces in the southern half of Vietnam could either disarm or relocate to the north. In Cambodia, nationalist and Communist forces were expected to disarm, but many Khmer Communists instead went into exile in North Vietnam.

King Sihanouk hoped that his strong fight for independence from France and his ensuing declaration of Cambodian international neutrality would dampen any further armed rebellion against his rule. Sihanouk stuck to his word and resisted American efforts to gain influence in Cambodia. The United States was intent on fighting Communism throughout the world. Nationalists and Communists in Cambodia were bent on resisting American involvement, which to them was a new form of colonialism, dressed up as Cold War politics.

King Norodom Sihanouk fought for independence from France while resisting American anti-Communist influence on Cambodian rule.

Average Cambodians, including many Democrats, gradually made their peace with Sihanouk's rule, and he actually began to enjoy widespread popularity. The KPRP and ICP lost much of their momentum, no longer able to harness widespread Cambodian anger and recruit Khmer fighters. Many Khmer Communists decided they had achieved the most important goals of Cambodian independence and simply returned to their ordinary lives.

Even Saloth Sar appeared to reenter conventional life, marrying a woman named Khieu Ponnary and becoming a schoolteacher at a private college in Phnom Penh. He was by all accounts a warm, gentle, encouraging, and supportive instructor. Yet at the very same time, Saloth Sar began to use his revolutionary pseudonym "Pol." He was working actively with the ICP to build a bigger and better Cambo-

Khieu Ponnary was the first Cambodian woman to earn a bachelor's degree. She was a teacher and helped her husband, Saloth Sol, with his revolutionary plans.

dian Communist Party, drawing mainly on the urban elite, including students, teachers, and Buddhist monks. Like many other urban-elite Khmer Communists, Saloth Sar had not given up the fight. He had merely gone underground and was biding his time.

CHAPTER 3

THE KHMER ROUGE ON THE RISE

The North Vietnamese Communists were very busy in 1960, between attacking the American-supported government in South Vietnam and convincing the Laotian and Cambodian Communists to help them in their efforts. In hopes of moving this collaboration along, they funded a party conference, which resulted in the formation of the Revolutionary Workers' Party of Kampuchea. Later it would be known by many names: the Communist Party of Kampuchea, the Cambodian Communist Party, the Red Khmers (as Norodom Sihanouk called them), or, in French, the Khmer Rouge. It was hoped that the group would appear to be a self-governing, independent party, but North Vietnam was a heavy supporter by way of direction and supervision early on.

VIETNAMESE CONTROL

In 1962, Saloth Sar became acting secretary of the party's Central Committee while still leading his respectable life as a married schoolteacher in Phnom Penh. Following an especially harsh police crackdown against the Cambodian Communist Party, however, Saloth Sar opted to leave Phnom Penh, abandoning his "cover" as a schoolteacher to flee to eastern Cambodia. Once there, he began working in a Vietnamese military camp at the border of Cambodia and Vietnam.

For the next seven years, Saloth Sar and his fellow Cambodian Communist militants lived in remote corners of eastern and northeastern Cambodia, shuttling between rebel camps and existing under the thumb of Vietnamese Communists. The North Vietnamese kept their Cambodian counterparts unarmed. The only weapons they had were those they were able to capture from Sihanouk's forces. Unable to wage armed warfare and restricted in their movements by their Vietnamese masters, the Cambodian Communists mostly served as scouts, guards, laborers, and "gofers."

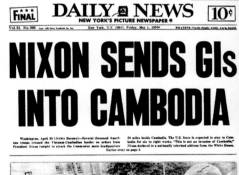

CONVENIENT COOPERATION

Meanwhile, American involvement in the growing war in Vietnam was escalating, first with military observers and then fighting soldiers deployed in ever-increasing numbers. As Vietnamese Communists began to take shelter

In 1970, U.S. president Richard Nixon sent troops into Cambodia. They bombed Cambodia after Vietnamese Communists fled there.

more often in Cambodia, American bombing raids along the Vietnam-Cambodia border became more frequent. Cambodian civilian casualties were high. Rural Cambodians were outraged and blamed Sihanouk, believing that the bombing was occurring with his blessing. The ranks of Cambodian Communist members swelled dramatically, and armed rebellion increased. The country was dissolving into chaos as both a Cambodian civil war and a Vietnam-American war were being waged on Cambodian territory simultaneously. The chief of Sihanouk's police force, Lon Nol, sensed impending disaster. Seeing a political opportunity as well, he conspired against his boss and removed Sihanouk from power in a bloodless coup in March 1970.

Always a wily and opportunistic political operator, Sihanouk, in exile in China, forged an alliance of convenience with his former Communist enemies. Together he, his loyalists, and the Cambodian Communists would form a National Liberation Front, allied with Vietnamese Communists and trained and supplied by Vietnamese armed forces. The goal was to overthrow the treacherous and harshly repressive Lon Nol, who was almost universally despised by Cambodians of every background.

Saloth Sar reemerged from the shadows to assume military leadership of this new alliance. As chief of the military directorate of the National Liberation Front, Saloth Sar gladly accepted Vietnamese training and weaponry. Looking toward the future, however, he sought to create a more self-sufficient corps of Khmer fighters who would not be indebted to or dependent upon Vietnamese masters. He began recruiting, educating, and training young Phnom Penh residents, mostly of the intellectual classes (teachers, students, and degree-holding professionals).

Yet over time, he began to hold up the ideal of the Cambodian peasant and laborer. He came to insist that Khmer Communist Party members should be drawn from these ranks, rather than from an intellectual class often "tainted" by associations with privilege, European elitism, and the monarchy. His goal was to establish a new society based upon Communist principles of communal ownership of land, collective work, and the nobility of the peasant and laborer. He intended to demolish the class system, mainly by forcibly converting or destroying members of the upper classes to which he himself belonged and owed his success.

THE KHMER ROUGE SURGES AHEAD

With Vietnamese training, arms, direction, and manpower, the rebellion against Lon Nol went well, resulting in the gaining of control over much rural territory throughout Cambodia by the increasingly Communist-dominated National Liberation Front. Lon Nol's forces shrank back and hunkered down in Phnom Penh and other cities. Saloth Sar seized the opportunity offered by this relative calm to preach Communist revolution throughout the nation, recruit among peasants and workers, and force the people of the villages he controlled to adopt his social and political policies.

THE KHMER ROUGE'S GENOCIDAL REIGN IN CAMBODIA

The United States began to believe that the Vietnam War was not winnable and that the former Indochina was probably lost to Communism. It decided to remove troops as quickly as it could and negotiated a cease-fire with North Vietnam. The Khmer Rouge refused to stop fighting in Cambodia, however. It felt outraged and betrayed that Vietnam, having achieved its goals in its own country, was now so willing to abandon the

In 1973, Lon Nol's army, supported by American bombers, fought back the Khmer Rouge in Phnom Penh, Cambodia.

fight for Communist victory in Cambodia. Saloth Sar decided the Khmer Rouge would fight on, alone if necessary.

With no cease-fire in place in Cambodia, the United States took parting shots at the Communist enemy by again heavily bombing Cambodia. Some two million Cambodian refugees fled the firestorm, their homes, villages, and farms destroyed. Once the bombing ceased, in less than six months, the Khmer

Rouge gained large numbers of new recruits, traumatized and embittered by the American bombing. The Khmer Rouge had swelled from a ragtag force of about three thousand men in 1970 to about sixty thousand men and women by 1973. It had also become far better armed and better trained. Saloth Sar decided that the time was right to at long last emerge from the countryside to swarm Phnom Penh and seize the seat of government.

PHNOM PENH COLLAPSES

The Khmer Rouge's newly effective and dangerous fighting force launched a series of attacks upon Phnom Penh from 1973 to 1975. The first two assaults were beaten back by Lon Nol's army. In late 1974, Saloth Sar's Khmer guerrillas surrounded Phnom Penh, seized the roads leading into and out of it, and mined the Mekong River. Then they began an artillery bombardment of the city. Lon Nol fled the city and went into exile. On April 17, 1975, Khmer Rouge troops marched into the capital to a joyous welcome.

Most residents of Phnom Penh believed that the Khmer Rouge victory would mark the end of war, the restoration of Sihanouk, and the return of peace and stability. Yet Norodom Sihanouk was now Cambodia's leader in name only. He was forcibly sidelined and kept in exile by Saloth Sar, who named himself "Comrade Secretary" and appointed twelve other men and women as various ministers and cabinet secretaries. These were the true leaders of a nation rechristened Democratic Kampuchea (DK), a country with a new name that was about to be radically transformed. Even the flow of Cambodian history was to be redirected, as Saloth Sar proclaimed it to be "Year Zero" for Democratic Kampuchea.

A parade of trucks celebrates the end of the war, carrying the triumphant Khmer Rouge past excited residents.

The Phnom Penh residents who were in the streets celebrating the Khmer Rouge victory did not know that Saloth Sar had already crafted a plan for what to do with the "enemies" of his Communist movement, nor did they know that they were now considered party enemies. Any residents of urban areas formerly controlled by Lon Nol who had not left their cities to join the Khmer Rouge were now viewed as traitors.

Cambodians try to climb the fences of the French embassy in Phnom Penh, where they hope to find safety from Pol Pot's order of evacuation.

During the siege of Phnom Penh, Saloth Sar decided that these enemies would be forcibly removed from the cities, marched into the countryside, and put to work. Khmer Rouge propaganda claimed that this would be ennobling work for these corrupt intellectuals and capitalists. It would make them good Khmer peasants. In reality, however, Saloth Sar, who soon began referring to himself as Pol Pot, was about to transform the Cambodian countryside into a massive forced-labor camp, political prison, and execution chamber. The cheering crowds who greeted Khmer Rouge troops that day in April could not possibly conceive of the deadly nightmare that was about to be visited upon them.

CHAPTER 4

A MADMAN AND HIS GENOCIDE

Cambodians who had lived in the cities and had failed to move to the country to join the Khmer Rouge before Pol Pot ascended to power found themselves in a very new situation. It didn't matter whether or not they were Khmer. Now they were called "new people" and "April 17 people." Meanwhile, the Khmer Rouge looked more fondly on the small farmers and other workers, or the "old people" or "original Khmers," who had battled and prevailed over the French, the Americans, and the monarchy. As far as the Khmer Rouge militants were concerned, the city people had lived a sheltered, privileged life while the country people had suffered and even died.

PHNOM PENH "PURGED"

Following the Khmer Rouge victory, the two million residents of Phnom Penh were told that an American bombing campaign was about to begin and that, for their safety, they must evacuate the city over two or three days. Many were robbed

On April 17, 1975, many Cambodians fled Phnom Penh after it was taken over and evacuated by the Khmer Rouge.

of the possessions they took with them, and their houses were looted. Goods that were thought to smack of elitism were particularly forbidden, such as wristwatches, jewelry, electronics, cars, motorcycles, and foreign currency. It was claimed that the party needed these things to help further the aims of the revolution and build up Democratic Kampuchea.

Bonfires were set to burn books, especially Buddhist teachings and French-language texts. Those who refused to leave their homes or part with their belongings were threatened with violence, beaten, and often shot. The evacuees were assured that the officials and armed forces of Democratic Kampuchea would look after their well-being. Yet as many as twenty thousand people died from hunger or exhaustion or were executed during the forced march to the countryside.

Upon reaching the villages to which they were assigned, each urban evacuee was required to write a brief autobiography, focusing on family background, youth and education, and profession. Most important, he or she had to account for his or her time during the Lon Nol regime. Each evacuee's immediate fate was decided by the content of his or her essay. Those with a background in the military, government, "elite" Western professions like engineering and architecture, and education (including schoolteachers and university students), or who had had foreign contact of any kind were sent away for "re-education." This usually meant they were executed. Sometimes, however, reeducation meant being sent to labor camps where starvation, torture, and interrogations were the daily routine. Skilled laborers were often sent back to the cities to get factories running again following the disruption of the Khmer Rouge takeover and the forced exodus of the urban population.

POL POT'S PLAN

Pol Pot's goal for Democratic Kampuchea was to achieve total self-sufficiency within four years. Pol Pot wanted to destroy Cambodia's traditional agricultural model of peasants laboring for a monarch or an urban elite. Instead, every Cambodian would now become a peasant and labor for the party and the nation, for the common good.

Laboring for the nation meant building it up and defending it against its historic enemies—France, Vietnam, and the United States. More generally, it meant defending it from weakness, dependency, and need. If Cambodia's agricultural industry could develop enough so that it could adequately feed the nation and provide trade income, then Cambodia would be able to beef up its industries. Never again, Pol Pot declared, would Cambodia be dependent upon other nations for anything it needed, including self-defense.

Pol Pot's regime scorned education and the more intellectual professions. High culture, including literature, was also frowned upon.

In order to throw all their effort and focus behind agricultural output, the vast majority of Cambodians would be relocated to cooperative farms and villages (which were basically labor camps). Private property and religion would be banned. Banking, money, and markets would be abolished and replaced with a barter system. Though its members were almost all European educated, the DK leadership prized illiteracy and de-emphasized education. It also treated high culture—including literature, art, dance, music, and Buddhist art and teachings—with hostile contempt. Hospitals, schools, and factories were closed. Buddhist monks were stripped of their robes and forced to labor in the rice fields. Families were intentionally separated, with infants removed from parents as soon as they were finished breast-feeding. It was believed that this would help insure that people viewed the DK as their family and would work hard for it, rather than for personal goals. All sentiment, attachment, and passion would now be directed to Democratic Kampuchea.

THE KILLING FIELDS

In this crazed push to move Democratic Kampuchea forward, millions of Cambodians suddenly found themselves laboring to clear forests, create and irrigate rice fields, build dams, and plant and harvest rice. Every element of their lives was controlled by cadres, or officials, of the village cooperative to which they had been assigned.

The cadres were backed up by soldiers who were often only in their teens. Illiterate, uneducated sons and daughters of rural peasants, many of these youths had been traumatized

Millions of Cambodians were made to perform hard labor, such as clearing forests, building dams, and planting crops. Their lives were controlled in almost every way.

by a childhood of civil war and American bombings. Their fear and anger were harnessed by Pol Pot, who also filled them with class and racial hatred for those "tainted" by non-Khmer traits, such as the possession of higher education, a foreign language, or minority ethnicity. Cadres and their soldiers understood that while the DK leadership was not troubled by excessive violence, it was enraged by leniency toward perceived enemies. Therefore, they frequently erred on the side of murderous repression, if only to save their own lives.

Under strict commands from DK's leadership, rice yields were expected to triple. In order to meet these obligatory targets, local commanders overworked the laborers. They worked fourteen- to eighteen-hour days, were fed a few tablespoons of watery rice a day, and lived in heavily guarded labor camps. "Old people"—the peasants who lived in the rural areas held by Communists before the fall of the Lon Nol regime—were given more and better rations and better living quarters, and they were allowed to join the army, the party, and their village's governing committee. "New people"—city dwellers evacuated to the countryside following Pol Pot's victory—were fed less, were punished more, had no rights, and were far more likely to be executed.

Death rates among "new people" were far higher than those of "old people." In many villages, rice harvests were too small to adequately feed all the new arrivals. Malaria and leeches were common, and as many as half a village's workers could be idled by sickness. Only those who worked a full day received their ration of rice. Missing one's daily production goals meant receiving less food, more work, or both. Hunger and disease became a vicious downward spiral. Sometimes disease and incapacity were viewed as anti-party rebelliousness, and the ill person was executed as an enemy of Democratic Kampuchea.

Yet, as time went on, unrealistic harvest goals were not met, hunger increased, and the "old people" began to suffer mistreatment and deprivation nearly as much as the "new people." Starving peasants foraged for lizards, snails, crabs, spiders, and wild vegetables. A cooperative village might suffer three or four dozen deaths a day. Gravediggers were reported to be dropping dead while burying the dead. Those who made mistakes, missed their production goals, were too ill to work, or accidentally broke farm equipment were often executed by electrocution, beheading, or butchering of the body.

Within three years of Pol Pot's reorganization of Cambodian society, hundreds of thousands of Cambodians were dying from starvation, malnutrition, overwork, poor or non-existent medical care, and execution in the so-called Killing Fields. In order to conserve bullets, people were often beaten to death with farm implements, like axes, shovels, hoes, and spades. The clothes of those who died were removed from the bodies and given to others to wear. If not buried in shallow mass graves, corpses were left in fields to fertilize the soil or they were burned in order to extract fertilizing phosphate from the bones' ashes.

The Cambodian Killing Fields were littered with the bodies and bones of people who died of disease, poor nutrition, or were executed.

THE STORIES OF CAMBODIAN CHILD SURVIVORS

Pol Pot was so successful in creating a closed society and in isolating Cambodia from the rest of the world that news of the ongoing genocide rarely leaked beyond the nation's borders. The world gradually became aware of the Khmer Rouge's atrocities following the eventual Vietnamese defeat of Pol Pot in 1979, as survivors' stories became known. Dith Pran, himself a survivor of Khmer Rouge death camps and the inspiration for the important 1984 film *The Killing Fields*, collected many Cambodian children's stories.

Seath K. Teng, aged four when the Khmer Rouge took over: "The Khmer Rouge soldiers told us not to love our parents or to depend on them because they are not the ones who supported us. They told us to love the new leaders and to work hard...If we didn't...,we would get a severe beating for punishment..."

Gen L. Lee, aged seven when the Khmer Rouge took over: "All I knew for over three years was that hunger and death were forever present. I ate creatures and wild fruits and vegetables that I would not have eaten during better times. I was not good at catching field rats and frogs. Snails, crabs, and tiny fish were easier to catch and hide."

Roeun Sam, aged fourteen when the Khmer Rouge took over: "They...had me ...watch the cows...One day...I noticed that a few of my cows were missing. I smelled something like a dead animal...[T]he cows were licking the dead body's clothes...You could see her long black hair and the string around her hands. I looked around and saw people who had been shot and their heads were smashed in."

Ing Pech was one of the few known survivors of the brutalities at Tuol Sleng prison, where thousands of Cambodians were tortured and killed.

IMPRISONED AND TORTURED AT S-21

The suffering and death were not limited to the countryside. Though Phnom Penh was largely emptied, one sector of it was still humming with activity. The Tuol Sleng interrogation facility, housed in a former school, was often the final destination for anyone Pol Pot deemed an enemy of Democratic Kampuchea. Also known as S-21, this facility was essentially a torture chamber and execution hall, ruled by the commandant Kaing Guek Eav, known as "Duch." More than fourteen thousand people were brought to S-21.

Only about six or seven are believed to have survived their interrogation and imprisonment.

The prisoners were isolated, forced to be silent, shackled to the floor, hosed down in large groups only every few days, and fed a handful of watery rice every day. They became malnourished and sick, and many died before, during, or after interrogation. Torture tactics included electric shocks, cigarette burns, hanging upside down, forced ingestion of urine or feces, having fingernails pulled out, water immersion, suffocation, and beatings with sticks and electric wire.

Initially, the prisoners were military and government personnel associated with Lon Nol's administration. As Pol Pot became more and more paranoid, the definition of "enemy" was broadened to include any Cambodian who had studied abroad (just as Pol Pot and most of the DK leadership had) or had any contact with foreigners, Khmer Rouge deserters, and ethnic Khmers who had been living in Vietnam, including Khmer Communists trained and educated by the Viet Minh. These were considered "external" enemies, people who were in direct opposition to the DK's Communist agenda. Those who were viewed as "pollutants" to the purity of the Khmer were also killed, including homosexuals; ethnic Vietnamese, Chinese, Thais, and Laotians; tribal minorities; and Buddhists, Christians, and Muslims. Even those who wore eyeglasses (which were taken as a sign of dangerous intellectualism or elitism) were killed.

Later in his increasingly erratic and desperate rule, the "enemies" became internal, as Pol Pot began to imagine himself surrounded by would-be traitors who were actually party members in good standing, some of them quite high ranking. Dragged in on charges ranging from poor agricultural production and sabotage to rebellious conspiracies and assassination attempts (probably more imagined than real), these Communist Party prisoners, like all the others at S-21, were interrogated, tortured, forced to write and sign phony confessions, and then executed. Bodies were buried in a cemetery on the property or in nearby fields.

In the end, at least 1.7 million Cambodians—ethnic Khmers and ethnic minorities, "old people" and "new people," Communists and non-Communists, men, women, and children—died during Pol Pot's reign. About 200,000 of these were executions; the rest were due to torture, starvation, overwork, and related disease. Though his reign of terror lasted less than five years, one-fifth of the country's population was decimated. Due to the extremely closed society Pol Pot had created, the world was mostly unaware that any of this devastation was occurring. Pol Pot would soon be swept from power, but he would escape justice and live hidden for many years in the country he all but destroyed.

CHAPTER 5

UNTHINKABLE CHAOS, THEN CALM

P ractically as soon as he ascended to command, Pol Pot decided that Cambodia must be cleansed of any influence from Vietnam. Any Khmers who had resided and trained in Vietnam were killed, and the few Vietnamese who were living in Cambodia were attacked. But particularly pivotal was his decision to instigate assaults on the borders of Vietnamese territory, in addition to bombarding villages. When Vietnam retaliated, the onslaughts grew more numerous and potent.

THE KHMER ROUGE FALLS

As Cambodia continued to pester Vietnam at its borders, ethnic Cambodians in southern Vietnam grew rebellious. Vietnam decided to nip this growing problem in the bud. Beginning in late 1977, Vietnam began deeper invasions of Cambodian territory, capturing both prisoners and towns and cities. After withdrawing, Vietnam offered peace negotiations, but Pol Pot went on a rampage instead, shelling border towns, burning villages, and slaughtering Vietnamese civilians. Tit-for-tat attacks continued until Christmas Day 1979, when Vietnam launched a massive invasion of Cambodia, involving heavy artillery, tanks, fighter jets, and helicopters.

Within two weeks, Vietnam reached Phnom Penh. Pol Pot's worst fears had come true, even if he had been the one to provoke the nightmare. The ancient enemy Vietnam was in firm control of his nation, and very real enemies now surrounded him. Pol Pot fled by helicopter and embarked on an eleven-year exile. Unrepentant and unyielding, he would continue to fight from a remote corner of the nation he once ruled and terrorized and live to escape punishment for his crimes.

Pol Pot leads the Cambodian army in 1979, attacking and burning towns bordering Vietnam and slaughtering Vietnamese people, even after Vietnam proposed peace negotiations.

As Vietnamese forces swept in, Khmer Rouge cadres and soldiers scattered. Many of them were killed in the fighting or died of disease and malnutrition as they hid in malaria-infested forests. Since the invasion halted the rice harvest, the long years of famine only worsened for Cambodia's beleaguered population, and thousands more died.

Vietnam set up a Communist puppet government, called the People's Republic of Kampuchea (PRK). It was mainly run by Khmer Communists who had fled to Vietnam before or during the Pol Pot reign and had not been Khmer Rouge members. Within two years, the Vietnamese had reintroduced money, markets, schools, hospitals, Buddhist practices, and family farming (as opposed to collective, cooperative farming).

AMERICAN BACKING

Still smarting from its defeat in Vietnam, the United States refused to recognize the PRK and instead supported Pol Pot and his still numerous Khmer Rouge troops, who were mostly exiled in Thailand. It did so despite the stories of Pol Pot's Cambodian genocide, which were finally beginning to be told to the outside world. The Khmer Rouge also received assistance from China, which was angered over Vietnam's close association with the Soviet Union, and Thailand, which feared a similar Vietnamese invasion.

The PRK put Pol Pot on trial in absentia (without his presence) and sentenced him to death, but Thailand declined to hand him over, and the United States refused to pressure it to do so. Once again, Pol Pot, despite his claims of independence and self-reliance, had benefited from the patronage of more powerful masters who were exploiting him for their own purposes.

Instead of forcing Pol Pot to face justice, the United States formed and sponsored a government-in-exile led by a dysfunctional coalition of former Democratic Kampuchea officials (and, therefore, high-ranking Khmer Rouge leaders), Norodom Sihanouk (who was living in China), and a former non-Communist Cambodian prime minister named Son Sann. The United States, China, and Thailand all offered this government financial assistance, and China provided its forces with arms.

Most of the coalition government's forces were Khmer Rouge. They were unable to recapture any significant portion of Cambodian territory, but the funding and weaponry allowed them to continue to wage war and evade punishment for humanitarian crimes for another two decades. It also allowed the Khmer Rouge to heavily mine western Cambodia, resulting in the death or maiming of thousands of more Cambodians throughout the 1980s and 1990s. Traumatized Cambodians continued to live in terror of Pol Pot's possible return to power.

A MADMAN FALLS APART

By 1989, Vietnam had wearied of the Cambodian situation

NEVER FORGET

In 1980, the Tuol Sleng prison was transformed into a museum, now called the Tuol Sleng Museum of Genocidal Crimes. In addition to its archive of four thousand coerced confessions and documents describing the prison's torture and interrogation practices and the daily life of prisoners and employees, the museum also houses hundreds of photographs of Tuol Sleng victims. Upon admittance to the prison, each prisoner was carefully posed and photographed. These are the final records of their last moments on earth.

Tuol Sleng prison, or S-21, is now known as the Tuol Sleng Museum of Genocidal Crimes, a reminder of the past and a memorial to the dead.

The prison's chief photographer, Nhem En, was called before the tribunal trying former Khmer Rouge officials for war crimes. Nhem En described his experiences to Seth Mydans, a *New York Times* reporter, in October 2007: "They came in blindfolded, and I had to untie the cloth...I was alone in the room, so I am the one they saw. They would say, 'Why was I brought here? What am I accused of? What did I do wrong?'" On November 1, 2007, he testified against Nuon Chea, believed to be the architect of the Khmer Rouge imprisonment and execution policies, and Kaing Guek Eav ("Duch"), the prison's commandant. "I realised that many times they arrested people who had done nothing," he told Thomas Bell in an article for the *Age.* "People from my village confessed to being in the CIA."

and withdrawn its troops. In 1991, an interim government to be supervised by the United Nations was agreed upon. Free elections to choose a new national government were scheduled, and all factions in the ongoing Cambodian war were to be disarmed. Pol Pot and the Khmer Rouge, however, refused to either disarm or participate in elections. The Royalist Party won the elections, returning King Norodom Sihanouk to the throne, though the position was purely ceremonial now. The Royalists entered into a coalition government with a party of former PRK officials. They soon declared the Khmer Rouge an illegal organization.

From its stronghold in western Cambodia along the Thai border, the Khmer Rouge continued to launch attacks, particularly against Vietnamese populations still in Cambodia. Pol Pot seemed to be descending into new depths of paranoia and madness. He ordered the execution of several of his leading and most loyal cadres, including his old friend and security chief Son Sen and Sen's wife and children. Mass defections from the Khmer Rouge began, including another of Pol Pot's oldest friends, Ieng Sary, a Parisian colleague and his former foreign minister.

Other leading Khmer Rouge cadres, fearing they would be executed next, decided to denounce and arrest Pol Pot. In July 1997, he was charged with treason by these leaders and put on trial in their jungle hideout. Most people felt this was a "show trial," designed only to improve the standing of the Khmer Rouge in international circles. If they could offer up Pol Pot for sacrifice, maybe they themselves would be spared punishment by Cambodian courts or international human rights tribunals.

A frail and ailing Pol Pot was sentenced to house arrest. He would die ten months later, unrepentant. In a series of interviews with journalist Nate Thayer, he insisted his conscience was clear, even though he "did some things against the people." On April 15, 1998, Pol Pot passed away under armed guard. The Khmer Rouge effectively died with him.

Cambodians reacted with a bewildered combination of relief, joy, anger, and wary disbelief. "I don't want to believe that he's dead, and I don't have time in my life to believe Khmer Rouge propaganda anymore," Youk Chang, director of the Documentation Center of Cambodia, an organization that has collected genocide evidence for eventual use at a hoped-for human rights tribunal, commented to Keith B. Richburg of the *Washington Post*. Chang, a former political prisoner of the Khmer Rouge, went on: "If he's dead, hand over his body to the people, don't just take photographs. I want to see him handcuffed and pushed into a jail, like his cadres did to me 20 years ago."

Pol Pot died convinced that everything he did, he did for Cambodia and its people, and that there would no longer even be a Cambodia had he not risen to power. Pol Pot was a product of privilege, foreign education, and Vietnamese training. He set out to murder people who shared this very same background. In addition to these "new people" he exterminated and the members of ethnic minorities he ordered slaughtered, however, Pol Pot also destroyed the very Khmers he held up as an ideal—the uneducated Cambodian peasant. His radical reorganization of Cambodian society spun out of control as he began to imagine enemies everywhere he looked. His utopian vision curdled into genocide and autogenocide.

PRESENT-DAY CAMBODIA

Today, thanks to international aid, Cambodia is slowly begin-

MAKING PEACE WITH THE PAST

In the summer and fall of 2007, five leading officials of the Khmer Rouge were arrested by Cambodian authorities and imprisoned. The five former members of Pol Pot's inner circle were Khieu Samphan, Khmer Rouge president and Pol Pot's "Brother Number Two"; Nuon Chea, Pol Pot's right-hand man and mastermind of the Khmer Rouge's prison and execution policies and practices; Kaing Guek Eav ("Duch"), the commandant of the Tuol Sleng prison; Ieng Sary, the Khmer Rouge foreign minister and Parisian colleague of Pol Pot; and his wife, Ieng Thirith, social affairs minister and sister of Pol Pot's wife. They were all charged with war crimes relating to the Cambodian genocide and tried by a tribunal established by the United Nations that includes both Cambodian and international judges.

In the past, Ieng Sary distanced himself from a decision-making role in the Khmer Rouge genocide. In a November

Continued on next page

Continued from previous page

13, 2007, *New York Times* article, Ieng Sary was quoted as saying in 1996, "Pol Pot made all decisions on all matters by himself...[Pol Pot] killed people without careful consideration." Similarly, Duch has pointed the finger at Nuon Chea for the atrocities committed in Tuol Sleng. For his part, Nuon Chea shrugs off any responsibility and seems prepared to meet his fate calmly: "I will read books in prison, learn another language, and exercise. I will do all of this so that I can make myself strong. I told my wife not to visit me in jail and, if I die, not to make a ceremony but keep the money for my children's education. When I die, it will all be finished."

In July 2010, Kaing Guek Eav was convicted. According to an article by Seth Mydans for the *New York Times*, his sentence stated that he was guilty of "war crimes and crimes against humanity and sentenced him to 35 years in prison for overseeing the torture and killing of more than 14,000 people. The court reduced that term to 19 years because of time already served and in compensation for a period of illegal military detention." Many Cambodians felt this was a light sentence that would possibly allow him to go free one day. Ieng Sary died in 2013 before a judgment was made. His wife, Ieng Thirith, who was the social affairs minister for the Khmer Rouge, was declared "unfit to stand trial." In 2014, both Nuon Chea and Khieu Samphan were convicted of crimes against humanity. Their lawyers planned to appeal, one of whom stated, "It is unjust for my client. He did not know or commit many of these crimes," according to an article for the BBC. In 2015, the Cambodian government pledged $4 million to fund the Khmer Rouge trials.

ning to rebound economically, though it is still burdened by political corruption. Norodom Sihanouk's son, Norodom Sihamoni, is now the ceremonial king, but Cambodia is a multiparty democracy with a prime minister and a Parliament.

The population is now overwhelmingly youthful. The great majority of Cambodians were born after the Khmer Rouge genocide, and the national sense of trauma is beginning to gradually heal. This process has been helped along by the formation of a special court that was created with assistance from the United Nations to bring the surviving Khmer Rouge leadership to justice. This tribunal, led by three Cambodian and two foreign judges, may be able to finally administer some justice to those Khmer Rouge leaders most responsible for the national bloodletting.

Pol Pot, however, will remain forever beyond justice. The world mourns for the almost two million Cambodians he and his henchmen killed, but the only sentence passed upon him was his nation's utter joy at his death. In this sense, history has passed its harshest judgment upon the man who became Pol Pot.

1925 Saloth Sar is born.

1930 The Indochina Communist Party (ICP) is founded and dominated by Vietnamese membership and leadership.

1940 France is conquered by Germany in the opening years of World War II. Germany offers control of Indochina to its Axis ally Japan.

1945 World War II ends with Germany and Japan's surrender. France regains colonial control of Cambodia after a brief period of quasi-independence.

1946 France grants limited political and constitutional freedoms to Cambodia. French troops battle ICP forces in northern Vietnam.

1947–1949 Saloth Sar graduates from College Sihanouk, fails university entrance exam, attends technical college, and receives radio-electricity engineering scholarship for study in Paris, France.

1951 The ICP encourages and sponsors the formation of the Khmer People's Revolutionary Party (KPRP), a supposedly independent Khmer Communist group that is in fact dominated by Vietnamese Communists.

1952 Saloth Sar joins the French Communist Party. King Norodom Sihanouk cracks down on Communists, declares martial law, dissolves the National Assembly, and rules by decree.

1953–1954 Saloth Sar returns to Cambodia and joins up with the ICP. The French grant Cambodia independence. Khmer Communists take up residence in North Vietnam.

1956 Saloth Sar, now married, becomes a schoolteacher but continues to work and recruit for the ICP.

1960 The Worker's Party of Kampuchea (WPK) is formed, and Saloth Sar is on its Central Committee. The name will later change to the Communist Party of Kampuchea (CPK). Sihanouk refers to these Khmer Communists as "Red Khmers," or Khmer Rouge.

1963 Saloth Sar goes into hiding and lives in a series of Communist Vietnamese military camps along the Cambodia-Vietnam border.

1970 Sihanouk is overthrown in a bloodless coup, and his former police chief, Lon Nol, rises to power. Sihanouk forms a United Front government with Communist forces to seek Lon Nol's defeat and his return to the throne. Saloth Sar becomes the chief of the front's military directorate.

1971–1972 Khmer Rouge forces receive training and arms from Vietnamese Communists and strengthen as a fighting force.

1973 The Khmer Rouge refuses a cease-fire agreed to by the United States and Vietnam. The United States heavily bombs Cambodian countryside, resulting in thousands of new recruits for the Khmer Communists.

1975 Khmer Rouge forces invade Phnom Penh and topple Lon Nol. Cambodia is renamed Democratic Kampuchea (DK). Saloth Sar emerges as the leader of DK and refers to himself as Pol Pot. The cities are evacuated, their residents forced to march into the countryside to be resettled in forced agricultural labor camps. Tens of thousands are executed or die during the march.

1975–1979 Genocide against ethnic and religious minorities, foreigners, intellectuals, ethnic Khmers, and others deemed to be "enemies" of DK is carried out. Almost two million

Cambodians die through overwork, disease, hunger, torture, or execution in prisons and agricultural labor camps.

1979 Repeated Khmer Rouge border attacks against Vietnam and Vietnamese populations in Cambodia prompt a Vietnamese invasion. Phnom Penh is captured, a Vietnamese-controlled Cambodian puppet government is established, and Pol Pot escapes into exile in Thailand.

1989–1993 Vietnam withdraws its armed forces from Cambodia. A UN-supervised provisional government rules Cambodia until elections can be held. The Khmer Rouge refuse to disarm. The Royalists win the election; Norodom Sihanouk returns as king, though the country's governing power now rests with the prime minister and Parliament.

1994–1997 The Khmer Rouge continue to launch small-scale attacks and mine western Cambodia. Pol Pot begins to execute leading and longtime Khmer Rouge officials. Mass defections from the Khmer Rouge begin. Remaining Khmer Rouge leaders arrest Pol Pot, put him on trial for treason, and sentence him to house arrest.

1998 Pol Pot dies.

2007 Five leading members of the Khmer Rouge are arrested, charged with war crimes and crimes against humanity.

2010 Kaing Guek Eav is convicted.

2013 Ieng Sary dies before a judgment is made.

2014 Nuon Chea and Khieu Samphan are convicted of crimes against humanity.

2015 Cambodian government pledges $4 million to fund the Khmer Rouge trials.

GLOSSARY

agrarian Relating to agriculture or ownership, division, and management of land.

annihilated Totally wiped out or eliminated; also defeated completely.

atrocity An act of brutality and cruelty.

autogenocide The mass murder of one's own citizens by a country's people or government.

Buddhism An Asian religion based upon the teachings of the sixth-century BCE Indian philosopher Siddhartha Gautama.

bureaucracy Managing of a government through a series of offices, departments, and agencies led by appointed officials and staffed by civil servants.

Cold War Political opposition between the western powers headed by the United States and the Soviet Bloc between 1945 and 1990.

collective Working together as a group; something that is worked on and achieved as a group.

colonies Bodies of people living in new territories that are governed by parent states.

Communism An economic theory or system based upon the belief of community ownership of all property; the belief in a classless society, to be achieved by revolution if necessary, in which all goods are shared out equally and the state plans all aspects of the national economy.

cooperative The owning of something by a group of members who share equally in the benefits and profits.

corruption A loss of integrity or moral values; acting improperly or illegally in order to gain something.

coup Short for "coup d'etat," a term describing the violent overthrow or alteration of an existing government by a group of rebels.

decimate To destroy.

elite The most distinguished, powerful, or well-regarded group.

empire A political entity that encompasses a large territory or group of territories and includes many different peoples, all united under a single, overarching governing structure.

exile A period of enforced or voluntary absence from one's home.

exterminated Killed or destroyed completely.

famine A severe shortage of food, often resulting in malnutrition and starvation.

guerrillas Small fighting forces of volunteer soldiers, often engaging in surprise attacks against much larger and better-organized government troops.

intellectual Someone engaged in educational pursuits; activities relating to the mind and its enrichment; someone from the educated class.

malaria A disease caused by a parasite that is transmitted by the bite of infected mosquitoes.

militia An army of citizens rather than professional soldiers, often formed in times of national emergency.

monarchy A system of government based upon the rule of a king or queen. The right to rule is passed down through the family, rather than through elections or appointments.

monk A man who withdraws from society, gives up his possessions, accepts poverty, joins a religious order, and devotes himself to mostly solitary religious devotion.

nationalist A member of a political party or group advocating national independence, autonomy, or strong national government.

overlord A ruler or master.

paranoia A mental disorder resulting in delusions, a sense of persecution, and constant suspiciousness.

privilege A special right, advantage, or benefit given to only some members of a society, usually the wealthy and ruling classes.

propaganda The systematic and widespread dissemination of ideas or doctrines to support one's cause or damage an opposing cause.

refugee A person who flees his or her home or country to seek shelter elsewhere.

sovereign Possessing independent authority.

subservient Ready to do what someone days without asking any questions.

taint To stain, infect, poison, pollute, or spoil.

utopian Describes a visionary scheme for the perfect society; an idealized place, state, or situation.

Cambodian Working Group
Montreal Life Stories Project
History Department
1455 de Maisonneuve Ouest
Montreal, QB H3G 1M8
Canada
Website: www.lifestoriesmontreal.ca/en/cambodia
  -working-group
This organization is made up of Cambodia's survivors, children of survivors, researchers, and students. They are dedicated "to the knowledge and the promotion of Cambodian culture, history and current events."

Crimes of War
1325 G Street NW, Suite 730
Washington, DC 20005
(202) 638-0230
Website: http://www.crimesofwar.org
The Crimes of War project is a collaboration of journalists, lawyers, and scholars dedicated to raising public awareness of the laws of war and their application to situations of conflict.

Genocide Watch
S-CAR, George Mason University
3351 North Fairfax Drive, MS4D3
Arlington, VA 22201
(202) 643-1405
Website: http://genocidewatch.net

Genocide Watch seeks to "predict, prevent, stop, and punish genocide and other forms of mass murder." The group wants to raise awareness and prevent genocide. Readers can read the latest news about the Cambodian genocide as well as others, both past and current.

Office of the United Nations High Commissioner for Human Rights (OHCHR)
Palais des Nations
CH-1211 Geneva 10
Switzerland
Website: http://www.ohchr.org
OHCHR is the principal United Nations office mandated to protect and promote human rights for all people.

United Human Rights Council (UHRC)
104 N. Belmont Street, Suite 313
Glendale, CA 91206
(818) 507-1933
Website: http://www.unitedhumanrights.org
UHRC seeks to call attention to those governments that distort, deny, and revise their own history to disguise past and present genocides, massacres, and human rights violations. UHRC campaigns include education, awareness, political activism, petition drives, and mainly consumer boycotts.

World Without Genocide
William Mitchell College of Law
875 Summit Avenue
St. Paul, MN 55105

(651) 695-7621
Website: http://worldwithoutgenocide.org/genocides-and
-conflicts/cambodian-genocide
World Without Genocide endeavors to keep people all over the globe safe. This organization also works against racism and prejudice with the aim of preventing genocide and making sure perpetrators pay for their crimes. They work to keep alive the memories of those who have suffered and lost their lives.

Yale University's Cambodian Genocide Program
P.O. Box 208206
New Haven, CT 06520-8206
Website: http://www.yale.edu/cgp
Since 1994, this program has aimed to learn as much as possible about the tragedy and to help determine who was responsible for the crimes of the Pol Pot regime.

WEBSITES

Because of the changing nature of Internet links, Rosen Publishing has developed an online list of websites related to the subject of this book. This site is updated regularly. Please use this link to access the list:

http://www.rosenlinks.com/BWGE/khmer

Des Chenes, Elizabeth, ed. *Genocide* (Contemporary Issues Companion). Farmington Hills, MI: Greenhaven, 2007.

Farish, Terry. *Either the Beginning or the End of the World.* Minneapolis, MN: Carolrhoda Lab, 2015.

Friedman, Mark D. *Genocide* (Hot Topics). Chicago, IL: Heinemann Library, 2012.

January, Brendan. *Genocide: Modern Crimes Against Humanity.* Minneapolis, MN: Twenty-First Century Books, 2007.

Koopmans, Andy. *Pol Pot* (Heroes and Villains). Farmington Hills, MI: Lucent Books, 2005.

Keat, Nawuth, and Martha Kendall. *Alive in the Killing Fields: The True Story of Nawuth Keat, a Khmer Rouge Survivor.* Washington, DC: National Geographic, 2009.

Kras, Sara Louise. *Cambodia: Enchantment of the World.* New York, NY: Children's Press, 2005.

Ngor, Haing, and Roger Warner. *Survival in the Killing Fields.* London, England: Constable & Robinson, 2012. Ebook.

Sheehan, Sean, and Barbara Cooke. *Cambodia* (Cultures of the World). New York, NY: Benchmark Books, 2007.

Sonneborn, Liz. *The Khmer Rouge.* New York, NY: Cavendish Square, 2012.

Springer, Jane. *Genocide* (Groundwork Guides). Toronto, ON: Groundwood Books, 2007.

Ung, Loung. *First They Killed My Father: A Daughter of Cambodia Remembers.* New York, NY: Harper Collins, 2010.

Weltig, Matthew S. *Pol Pot's Cambodia.* Revised edition. Minneapolis, MN: Twenty-First Century Books, 2012.

BBC. "Top Khmer Rouge Leaders Guilty of Crimes Against Humanity." BBC, August 7, 2014. Retrieved December 7, 2015 (http://www.bbc.com/news/world-asia-28670568).

Bell, Thomas. "Chilling Start to Khmer Rouge Tribunal." *Telegraph*, November 1, 2007. Retrieved December 8, 2015 (http://www.telegraph.co.uk/news/worldnews/1568068 /Chilling-start-to-Khmer-Rouge-tribunal.html).

Bell, Thomas. "Khmer Rouge 'Artist' Justifies Haunting Faces of Doomed." *Age*, November 3, 2007. Retrieved December 8, 2015 (http://www.theage.com.au/news /world/khmer-rouge-artist-justifies-haunting-faces-of-doomed/2007/11/02/1193619144986.html).

Chandler, David P. *Brother Number One: A Political Biography of Pol Pot.* Boulder, CO: Westview Press, 1999.

Chandler, David P. *Voices from S-21: Terror and History in Pol Pot's Secret Prison.* Berkeley, CA: University of California Press, 1999.

DePaul, Kim, ed. *Children of Cambodia's Killing Fields: Memoirs by Survivors.* New Haven, CT: Yale University Press, 1997.

Drennan, Justine. "40 Years After Cambodia Fell to the Khmer Rouge, Perhaps We Shouldn't Focus so Much on Anniversaries." *FP*, April 17, 2015. Retrieved December 7, 2015 (http://foreignpolicy.com/2015/04/17/40-years-after -cambodia-fell-to-the-khmer-rouge-anniversary-tribunal -phnom-penh).

Fuller, Thomas. "Couple Who Helped Lead Khmer Rouge Are Arrested." *New York Times*, November 13, 2007. Retrieved November 2007 (http://www.nytimes.com/2007/11/13 /world/asia/13cambo.html).

Kiernan, Ben. *How Pol Pot Came to Power: Colonialism, Nationalism, and Communism in Cambodia, 1930–1975.* 2nd ed. New Haven, CT: Yale University Press, 2004.

Kiernan, Ben. *The Pol Pot Regime: Race, Power, and Genocide in Cambodia Under the Khmer Rouge, 1975–79.* 2nd ed. New Haven, CT: Yale University Press, 2002.

Mydans, Seth. "Anger in Cambodia Over Khmer Rouge Sentence." *New York Times*, March 14, 2013. Retrieved December 7, 2015 (http://www.nytimes.com/2010/07/27/world /asia/27cambodia.html?_r=0).

Mydans, Seth. "Former Khmer Rouge Leader Arrested." *New York Times*, September 20, 2007. Retrieved October 2007 (http://www.nytimes.com/2007/09/20/world/asia /20cambodia.html).

Mydans, Seth. "Ieng Sary, Former Official of Khmer Rouge, Dies at 87." *New York Times*, March 14, 2013. Retrieved December 7, 2015 (http://www.nytimes.com/2013/03/15 /world/asia/ieng-sary-khmer-rouge-leader-tied-to -genocide-dies-at-87.html).

Mydans, Seth. "Out from Behind a Camera at a Khmer Torture House." *New York Times*, October 27, 2007. Retrieved October 2007 (http://www.nytimes.com/2007/10/26/world /asia/27cambo.html).

Pran, Dith, and Kim DePaul. *Children of Cambodia's Killing*

Fields: Memoirs by Survivors. New Haven, CT: Yale University Press, 2005

Richburg, Keith B. "Khmer Rouge Head Pol Pot Dies in Cambodia at Age 73." *Tech* (MIT), April 17, 1998. Retrieved November 2007 (http://www-tech.mit.edu/V118/N20/akhmer.20w.html).

Short, Philip. *Pol Pot: Anatomy of a Nightmare.* New York, NY: Henry Holt and Company, LLC, 2004.

Sokha, Cheang. "Gov't Pledges $4 Million More for KR Tribunal." *Khmer Times*, November 17, 2015. Retrieved December 7, 2015 (http://www.khmertimeskh.com/news/17912/gov---t-pledges--4-million-more-for-kr-tribunal).

INDEX

ABOUT THE AUTHOR

Zoe Lowery is an avid student of history, constantly reading and studying about the past and other thought-provoking topics. She has written and edited a number of books on the topic for Rosen Publishing. Lowery lives in Colorado.

Sean Bergin is a writer living in New York City who has written several books on government, politics, world leaders, and history. He has a master's degree in medieval literature, specializing in medieval Irish poetry. Through his study of Irish history, he has become keenly interested in other nations' experiences of colonialism and genocide.

PHOTO CREDITS

Cover (photo) Gerhard Joren/LightRocket/Getty Images; cover (cracked texture) Marbury/Shutterstock.com; p. 5 Anadolu Agency/Getty Images; p. 7 Globe Turner/Shutterstock.com; p. 8 John S. Lander/ LightRocket/Getty Images; p. 11 Howard Sochurek/The LIFE Picture Collection/Getty Images; p. 13 Jehangir Gazdar/Woodfin Camp/The LIFE Images Collection/ Getty Images; p. 16 Nat Farbman/The LIFE Picture Collection/Getty Images; p. 18 The Asahi Shimbun/Getty Images; pp. 19, 35 Pictures from History/Bridgeman Images; p. 21 New York Daily News Archive/Getty Images; pp. 24 - 25, 26 Roland Neveu/LightRocket/Getty Images; p. 27 SJOBERG/AFP/Getty Images; p. 29 AFP/Getty Images; p. 31, 37 John Bryson/The LIFE Images Collection/Getty Images; p. 33 Keystone-France/Gamma-Keystone/Getty Images; p. 41 Kurita Kaku/Gamma-Rapho/Getty Images; p. 44 Nigel Killeen/Moment/Getty Images; back cover, pp. 12, 15, 36, 37, 44, 47, 48 (skulls) rangizzz/Shutterstock.com; pp. 7, 13, 20, 28, 40 (top) pimchawee/Shutterstock.com; additional background textures Reinhold Leitner/ Shutterstock.com, © iStockphoto.com/ShutterWorx
Designer: Brian Garvey; Photo Researcher: Heather Moore Niver